HORSHAM
THEN and NOW

Horsham in the throes of redevelopment, 1989.

Tony Wales

Photographs: Bill Young

Previous Titles
Tony Wales
We Wunt be Druv (1976)
A Sussex Garland (1979)
The West Sussex Village Book (1984)
Sussex Customs, Curiosities and Country Lore (1990)
The Landscapes of West Sussex (1994)
Horsham and District in Old Photographs (1994)

Bill Young
Line of Fire – a History of Firefighting in Lewes (1996)
Lewes Then and Now (1998)

First published in 2000 by S B Publications
19 Grove Road, Seaford, Sussex BN25 1TP

ISBN 1 85770 202 6

Typeset by JEM Lewes

Printed by MFP Design & Print
Longford Trading Estate
Thomas Street
M32 0JT

ACKNOWLEDGMENTS

I am very grateful to the following who have helped with this book, either in providing old photographs or in sharing some of their memories:
John Cannon, Cecil Cramp, Frank Holmes, Horsham Museum and its curator Jeremy Knight, John Payne, Lens of Sutton, Hilda Wales, Minnie Wales, Ronald Wales, West Sussex Library Service, Martin Hayes, Robin Knibb.

BIBLIOGRAPHY and SOURCES

Albery, William: *A Millennium of Facts in the History of Horsham and Sussex 947-1947,* 1947
Burstow, Henry: *Reminiscences of Horsham,* 1911
Chapman, Brigid: *West Sussex Inns*, 1988
Horsham Society: *Horsham Pubs, Past and Present*
Horsham Society: *Horsham Town Trail,* 1993
Windrum, Anthony: *Horsham, an Historical Survey,* 1978
Other sources include the Official Guide to Horsham Shopping Week, 1910;
Pike's and Kelly's Directories of Horsham of various dates

INTRODUCTION

I was born and brought up in Horsham but, a few years ago, my wife and I moved to the coast for our retirement. Horsham, though, had cast its spell and in 1999 we returned – to a town more than a little changed from when we had left it. Therefore it seems appropriate that my first book after my return should be this Then and Now compilation.

My previous four books on the town consisted entirely of old pictures, but thanks to the splendid photographic work of Bill Young this new book looks not just at the old pictures, but as far as possible the same views today. Some are so different that it is hard to believe they are the same places; in other cases the views are almost unaltered.

Since the beginning of the 19th century Horsham has grown tremendously. A contributory factor was the coming of the railway in the mid-19th century, coupled with improved roads. Today it is a vibrant place with local industries and artistic and sporting activities all contributing to the changing face of Horsham.

As we move into a new century, this seems a most appropriate time to look back over the changes that many of us have lived through. Horsham, which was once a self-contained market town, has changed almost beyond our wildest anticipations. Many will still recall when the carriers came into the town regularly, bringing messages and shopping lists from the outlying villages. The roads were relatively uncongested, and a favourite Sunday evening occupation was to gather at the Black Horse corner to watch the gradually increasing traffic as it coped with the new fangled traffic lights.

We felt we knew everyone we met, or so it seemed, and the pace was definitely more leisurely. The shops were more often than not owned by local families and the coming of the 'big' stores like Timothy White and Woolworth set tongues wagging. Gradually as the twentieth century advanced, our first tiny cinemas gave way to the larger picture palaces, with names like Ritz and Odeon, until they too became outmoded.

There were other casualties such as the much loved Capitol Theatre, and St Mark's Church in North

Street. But the twentieth century marched on with an almost unimaginable period of reconstruction of the town centre. We could hardly believe what we were seeing, with whole vistas changing almost overnight. Eventually the dust settled and we are now left with a town with so many fine features that it has become an attraction for visitors from a wide area.

  My childhood in the Twenties and Thirties was not only in a very different town, but one could truthfully say in a completely different world. To an even greater extent my grandparents and parents, who also grew up in Horsham, would not recognise much of what we take for granted today, and it is to their memory that I dedicate this book.

Tony Wales, Horsham, 2000

Horsham in the Second World War;
roadblocks in Guildford Road.

A BAND CONCERT, IN CARFAX, HORSHAM.

THEN – CARFAX BANDSTAND: This picture dates from *c*1919, and shows the bandstand in its original position as it was built in 1891-1892. It was in regular use by the early 1900s, with local bands giving concerts usually on Sunday evenings. My mother remembered when the teenage girls and boys, dressed in the latest style, would assemble on the Carfax, sedately separated at the beginning of the evening. The trick was to catch the eye of the one you fancied, hoping that this would result in the boy walking the girl home at the end of the performance.

NOW: The bandstand has been moved a little to the left of its original site, although it still looks very smart. Local and visiting bands play there, usually on Saturdays, with a great variety of musical styles. Some of the new chunky street furniture provides useful seats. Many of the original shop fronts survive as a backdrop.

THEN – THE CARFAX, EAST SIDE: This 1905 picture shows the drinking fountain erected here in 1897 to commemorate Victoria's Jubilee. Many notables attended the opening ceremony, and it was considered a great step forward in providing drinking water for all who needed it. In 1977 it was resited in Copnall Way, and was subsequently given a facelift and moved for the second time to its present site at the junction of North Street and Chart Way. After the 1914-18 war Horsham War Memorial was erected in the empty space between the Jubilee Fountain and the bandstand. This was in 1921, and it remained there until being moved to its present position during the latest re-development. The spire of St Mark's Church in North Street can be plainly seen.

NOW: The drinking fountain has disappeared and the vehicles and road surfaces look very different. St Mark's spire may still be seen, although it is in a slightly different position and it lacks the main body of the church. Most of the buildings remain intact, although the attractive shop front (just below the spire) is a facsimile of the original in the earlier picture.

THEN – THE CARFAX, NORTH SIDE: The period is around 1900, the roadway has still to be embellished with islands, and the road surface leaves much to be desired. At this time the Carfax was only just past the era of open-air fairs and bonfires, when the Duke of Norfolk called it 'all that waste and unenclosed land'. The shop on the extreme right is number 44, Louis Cesare Pierre's antique furniture and bric-a-brac showrooms. My mother, who played with the Pierre offspring, remembered it as a veritable treasure house of mysterious delights. Much later in the 1945-50 period, it became a music and record shop, The Albion Music House, where on one evening a week I ran Horsham's first jazz club.

NOW. The same corner in 1999, but with added trees and a facsimile of the old Horsham stocks, erected by the Horsham Museum Society. These took the place of the pre-war stocks, which were retired to the museum at the start of hostilites (although probably these were also facsimiles, as the originals were said to have been burnt by some of the townsfolk after their use had gone out of fashion).

THEN – THE CARFAX, NORTH SIDE: This l920s picture shows one of the lamp standards provided for the Carfax by local councillor Nellie Laughton. Soon the Carfax was to become largely a bus interchange area, with the original open space filled by island pavements. These made ideal stopping places for the variety of buses that travelled to a great many destinations from Horsham. There were the small companies such as Rayners, Mitchells and Comfy Coaches, although the Southdown company with its familiar green and yellow livery provided the majority of services. One way traffic in the Carfax was introduced in 1928.

NOW: The roadway has gone and this part of the Carfax looks much larger, except when on Saturdays this area is filled with market stalls, adding a continental touch to the local scene. There have been post offices in the Carfax since the 1890s and the present General Post Office is on the left of this picture (although not open from 7am to 10pm as it was in earlier times).

THEN – THE CARFAX, WEST SIDE: A relatively modern view of two shops on the inner circle of the Carfax in 1954. The electricity showrooms, only recently nationalised at this time, sport the distinctive logo of the South Eastern Electricity Board. Previously the undertaking had been under the control of the Horsham Urban District Council, with the offices and works in Stanley Street. During the earliest years, the shop was merely a showplace for appliances, with the customers having to visit other local shops to make a purchase. Next door was the popular cooked-meat and provision shop of Mr J Streete, who even at this time was in to 'healthy' foodstuffs.

NOW: The two shops are still there, with the upstairs windows litle changed. However the type of business has altered, with houses and flats being offered instead of more portable commodities. One of the new 'Victorian' lamp posts shows off well in the foreground.

THEN – THE KING'S HEAD: The picture of a coach in front of this important hotel in the Carfax dates not from the eighteenth century, but from around 1904. The coach is one of several which were running at this time, in an attempt to revive the coaching era. Nostalgia played its part, but not strongly enough to keep the coaches on the roads more than a few years. The King's Head dates from the seventeenth century and has an eighteenth century facade. The picture shows off the roof of Horsham slabs (quarried not far from the town). In 1801 the hotel was also a post office, and in the 1850s became the local headquarters of the revenue men fighting the smugglers. Later it had its own horse bus, meeting the London trains.

NOW: The hotel has not changed its outside appearance too much, but garages take the place of the stables and coach yard. It now rejoices in the title of Ye Olde King's Head.

THEN – THE KING'S HEAD: A picture from Walser's Illustrated Guide of 1892 showing the East Street side of the building. Here were the King's Head Assembly Rooms, where many well known actors performed, and concerts were held. In its heyday the actors, who appeared in plays such as *Murder in the Red Barn,* paraded the town in costume, advertising their show. But this was not Horsham's first theatre; the first had been on the Carfax at the back of The Stout House pub (later the site of the Carfax Cinema).

NOW: The same view, although the old Assembly Rooms have now become part of the hotel's accomodation, having passed through a phase when they were known as The King's Dining Rooms. The attractive facade which included the original entrance to the theatre may still be seen.

THEN – WEST STREET, WEST END: This was Horsham's high street early in the century. Many old family businesses were found here, such as Albery the saddler, Hunts the drapers, and Jury Cramp the jeweller and optician. A 1910 guide said: 'In West Street will be found attractively dressed shops of almost every kind'. The picture shows the spot known as Black Horse Corner, named after the hotel affectionately termed the 'Old Kicker' by its patrons. The Corn Exchange was next door, later incorporated into the hotel. One way traffic was introduced into West Street in 1928. Later the flow was reversed, and this earned the nickname 'Barker's Bite', after the current police chief.

NOW: The same end of the street, dominated by the much-maligned Shelley Fountain. For those who see it for the first time, the fountain must come as something as a shock. Originally the design met with much criticism, but familiarity seems to have allowed it to become an accepted part of the local scene. The Black Horse Hotel has of course disappeared, with the name surviving, attached to the service road which now runs behind the shops on the south side

THEN – THE SWAN HOTEL: Half way along West Street on the north side was one of Horsham's many pubs (there were once fifty of them). This is a picture of it in the 1950s, although its history went back to coaching days, when the inn yard welcomed coaches that took four and three quarter hours travelling to London. The yard, which was a popular short cut from Albion Road to West Street, was closed one day a year to protect its private ownership. It once housed a number of small traders. Some readers may remember the newspaper seller outside who kept up a constant cry of what sounded like 'tar paper' (Star paper). The attractive stained glass on the front of the building was said to have been sold to a buyer in the USA when the pub closed.

NOW: Swan Walk, which replaced the old Swan Hotel, was Horsham's first shopping precinct – originally uncovered but later revamped and roofed. The little local shops in the old yard have now been replaced by such large multiples as Boots, Smiths, BHS and Marks and Spencer.

West Street, Horsham.

THEN – WEST STREET, EAST END: This was as it appeared in 1909, full of bustle and activity. Horsham's most important shops were here, with a number of interesting shop signs – a huge pair of spectacles (Jury Cramp, now in Horsham Museum), a golden boot, and a clock marking the Clock House Cafe with, above it, an eagle. Jury Cramp's shop, on the left side, also had wooden shutters which were put up each evening, and the last boot-scraper in Horsham. Hunts (drapers), Horsham's most prestigious shop was on the left corner, being replaced by Capital and Counties Bank, whilst Hunts remained next door at number 2. Opposite was Chart and Lawrence, also drapers, which had replaced George Duke's Emporium.

NOW: West Street is now pedestrian friendly, and the bank on the corner has become Lloyds TSB. Otherwise West Street remains full of interesting shops, although some of the biggest names have moved to Swan Walk.

THEN – THE TOWN HALL: This view is from *c*1930, with the point duty policeman on what was a fairly busy corner at this period. The building (now strangely known as the Old Town Hall, although Horsham does not have a new one), was built in its present form in 1888, on the site of an earlier market house. There are three panels on the frontage showing the Royal arms, and the arms of the Duke of Norfolk (who was responsible for the building), and the town. Once, Cramp's Temperance Hotel, run by that famous Horsham character Jury Cramp, was on the left of the Town Hall.

NOW: The Town Hall, little altered externally, but now used mainly for sales and meetings. The Market Square in front of the hall, is now pedestianised, and once again fills its original function as a place for market traders.

THEN – MIDDLE STREET: This is the east end of what must be Horsham's shortest and narrowest shopping street, and the first to be pedestrianised. For many years this corner had a chemists' shop on the right hand side; in this 1900 photo the proprietor was Robert Gallier, who had as his address 1 The Carfax. Later the chemist was H R Camplin, who also advertised himself as a supplier of medicated wines and fancy goods. Middle Street had a certain reputation for scuffles and arguments between carters who tended to meet in the middle, with no room for passing. And during the 1939-45 war Canadian tanks which were unwisely routed through this street, found their tracks jammed between the two opposite kerbs.

NOW: A very different view of this corner, with a bank replacing the old chemist's shop, and the roadway now uniformly paved, plus lots of attractive Victorian-style street furniture.

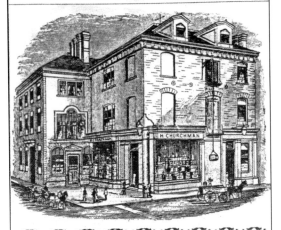

30

THEN – CORNER OF SOUTH STREET: Ask any-one where South Street begins and ends and quite likely they will be unable to tell you, as it is really a very short street which quickly merges into the Causeway. The old advertisement from early in this century shows the grocers shop of H Churchman, on the Middle Street-South Street corner. Note the small pedestrians in the drawing – obviously to make the building appear larger and more imposing. This was the name that my mother remembered, and even when it later changed to Evershed and Cripps (as in my childhood) she resolutely refused to call it anything but Churchmans. I remember it for the splendid display of expensive Christmas crackers in the left hand window each year.

NOW: The old building is still essentially intact, although now a building society office – a sign of the times, as is the 'remainder' bookshop next door. One thing happily still remains – the old crane, which is shown in use on the earlier picture. I remember how my day was made, when as a boy I was treated to the sight of this piece of nineteenth century machinery in action. Now it may not be in use, but at least someone had the common sense to allow this lovely reminder of old Horsham to remain intact.

Springfield Road, Horsham.

THEN – SPRINGFIELD ROAD: A tranquil picture from *c*1920. This shows the relatively new Roman Catholic Church of St John the Evangelist on the left, which had been built in 1919 by Father Bernard Cassidy. It replaced an earlier church of 1865 on the opposite side of the road, part of which can be made out in this photograph. This was sold in 1926 for £2,608 and became a furniture shop, with the upper part still showing its church-like exterior. The RC presbytery is the large building just before the church, on the left side of the road. At the southern end there was Seagrave's bakery on the left corner, with its tantalising aroma of new baked bread wafting up from basement windows beside the pavement.

NOW: The same road although difficult to recognise as it has been paved, and a large resturant now occupies the corner site. The old presbytery has gone, to be replaced by a new building – however the 1919 church is still intact.

THEN – LONDON ROAD: The Methodist Church (originally the Wesleyan Chapel) is the middle building. It was built in 1882 at a cost of little more than £2,000, replacing an earlier building of 1832. The modern Wesley Hall was built in 1975, taking the place of earlier huts. London Road was originally rather grand with a line of lovely houses on one side. Several townsfolk of note lived there, including Major Middleton, who built Horsham's Capitol Cinema, and the local historian (and saddler) William Albery. There were also a number of small cottages, plus a blacksmiths' and a wheelwrights'.

NOW: The Methodist Church is still there, but the old cottages have long disappeared, to be replaced by a car park. One of the fine old houses on the other side of the church has been put to commercial use, with modern shop-fronts.

THEN – POTTERS CORNER: This picture dates from the 1950s. Until recent times Horsham had several named corners, called after local traders or well known establishments; for instance, Black Horse Corner and Piggott's Corner. Potter was the name of the family who ran the shop where London Road met Springfield Road. I am unsure how far back the name went, but it was unfailingly spoken of in this way during my childhood. A pleasant memory is of stopping there with my parents for an ice cream, served in a small dish (rather than the usual cornet) as a special treat. In much earlier times this was the spot known for a very unpopular toll gate, which finally disappeared in the 1850s.

NOW: Although the houses in London Road appear little altered, the corner has undergone a massive change, with this unusual modern building dating from the l950s. After its initial occupancy, it remained empty for some while, but has now become a thriving video rental shop.

THEN – PARK STREET: Once known as Back Lane, this street ran from East Street to North Street, with a mixture of houses and shops. In the 1960s this section near the East Street end had the Park Hotel, plus some cottages (one of which had become the Citizens Advice Bureau), and a large building erected in 1873 as the Drill Hall for the Sussex Volunteer Force (from 1910 the Territorials). At the time of this photograph it had become a furniture store.

NOW: This section of Park Steet, re-named Park Place, has been sealed off at the North end. The Park Hotel building has become the Horsham Antique Centre, housing a host of treasures for the collector. The other buildings have disappeared, making way for an entrance to a new shopping area, and a small multi-storey car park.

THEN – EAST STREET: This is the part sometimes known as Upper East Street, as it looked in 1892. East Street was once Horsham's most important shopping street after West Street, although at the time of this picture the condition of the road surface left a lot to be desired. Many of the East Street shops were roofed with Horsham stone slabs, and at around this period the street boasted a jam factory. Pubs included the Beehive, which later became a newsagents, and on the opposite corner, The Horse and Groom, dating from the 1840s. This was subsequently renamed The Tut 'n' Shive, but has now reverted to its original name.

NOW: A big change, although the building on the corner still shows traces of its origins, and the chapel to its left also survives.

THEN – THE IRON BRIDGE: This photograph shows the railway bridge in Upper East Street, as it was in the early part of this century, with the Bridge House Hotel nearby. It seems always to have been viewed with some affection by the townsfolk, although it has been the scene of several mishaps over the years. The road was lowered when the bridge was built, hence the wall and high pavement on the left.

NOW: The bridge is still there, but looking a little different and with some large new buildings close by. The high pavement still survives, as does the house immediately to the left of the bridge; although it has had all its advertising matter removed.

QUEEN STREET HORSHAM.

THEN – QUEEN STREET: The scene as it was in the early 1900s. This was the continuation of the road after the Iron Bridge. Always the slightly less expensive side of the town, with lots of small shops such as William Clements the butcher, Burgess and Sons, blacksmiths, Susan Comber, corn dealer; Dewdney Brothers, builders and Arthur Goldsmith with his 'Fancy Repository'. The town gaol was in Queen Street, the site of Horsham's last public execution in 1844 (in the following year the gaol was demolished).

NOW: The same row of shops but with new owners and new kinds of businesses. Cars have taken the place of the horse drawn vehicles in the earlier picture.

THEN – THE QUEENS HEAD: An undated picture of the pub in Queen Street, but obviously in the nineteenth century, as this original building was demolished in 1900. In the stables on the right, in 1844, the body of John Lawrence, the last man to be publicly hanged in Horsham, was exhibited. The charge to view the corpse was twopence, and 3,000 were said to have taken advantage of the offer. In 1830, a local boy, Edward Smith, had been stabbed outside the inn by Harry Hewett, who was subsequently found guilty of manslaughter and transported to Bermuda.

NOW: The Queens Head as it is today. This is the new building, erected on the site of the old one, early in this century, at a cost of £1,000.

48

THEN – THE BAPTIST CHURCH: This was the original church in 1898, some four years after it was built, when this part of Brighton Road was known as East Parade. In 1923 a new building was erected on the same site, with an opening service followed by tea at ninepence a head. In the late 1920s older members of the Sunday School spent summer weekends in St Leonards Forest. A camp anthem was sung to the tune of *There is a Happy Land – We are the boys of HBC from Horsham way,/Where we get bread and jam three times a day./Eggs and bacon we don't see, nor much sugar in our tea,/We are gradually fading away.* But I feel sure they didn't.

NOW: The present day church, with an active congregation who celebrated their centenary in 1994.

THEN – NEW STREET, THE GARDENER'S ARMS: This picture dates from *c*1954, not so very long before the pub closed in the early 1970s. Once there had been fifty pubs in Horsham, when these estabishments were almost the only places of refreshment and recreation for the working man.

NOW: The same spot but much altered, with the pub replaced by modern flats. By a bright inspiration a similar sign has been retained for the flats. Latterly The Horsham historian, Frank Holmes, lived here, and I often had the pleasure of visiting him and discussing old Horsham times.

NEW STREET HORSHAM. 841.

THEN – UPPER NEW STREET: A neat line of typical pre-First World War houses, in the area often spoken of as 'back of the station'. The date of the photograph is *c*1914. The horse and cart and a man with a barrow are typical of the only wheeled traffic in those halcyon days before the Great War and the rest of the twentieth century changed our lives completely.

NOW: The houses remain, surprisingly little altered, although the same cannot be said concerning the traffic.

THEN – CAUSEWAY HOUSE: An undated picture, but probably early in this century. This lovely house dates from at least the fifteenth century, although there was certainly a house on the same site earlier than this. Since 1941 it has been the home of the Horsham Museum, which had been founded in 1893 by members of the Free Christian Church in Worthing Road, and then moved to Horsham Park.

NOW: Causeway House on a dark day, but showing the improvement in the surface of the roadway. This is one of Horsham's oldest streets, and the first one to have its houses numbered. Almost all the houses are interesting, and include some of the most ancient in the town.

PUMP ALLEY HORSHAM

THEN – PUMP ALLEY, THE CAUSEWAY: One of Horsham's many interesting old alleyways. The picture is undated, but is probably pre-1900. Another interesting Causeway twitten is Morth's Gardens, which is reached through a tunnel at the front of one of the houses. The Gardens are named after John Morth, a local carpenter, associated with "The Society of Independents." Both of these short cuts emerge in Denne Road.

NOW: The same alleyway, with little changed except the dress of the residents.

THEN – THE CAUSEWAY: An undated picture, but probably *c*1920. Earlier, around 1900, my mother remembered the roadway as being very muddy in winter, with paving stones from one side to the other at intervals. She remembered picking her way carefully down the street, to a house that sold pickles, which she was able take away in her mother's basin. Earlier still, in the seventeenth century, it is recorded that five loads of stones were provided for the Church Casey (they were unsure of the spelling in those days – sometimes it was Causie or Causy).

NOW: The same street, with not too much changed apart from the trees. Even the old lantern projecting from one of Horsham's oldest houses is still intact.

THEN – THE PARISH CHURCH OF ST MARY THE VIRGIN: The picture is from a nineteenth century book of prints. The much loved church is a blend of thirteenth, fourteenth and fifteenth century building. The restoration in 1864-1865 cost more than £8,000, and provided the beautiful seven-light east window which replaced an earlier window destroyed in a hurricane. The spire, with its slight lean to the south, is covered by 50,000 shingles, and the bells, which may be heard to their best advantage on a fine summer's evening, date from 1752.

NOW: The church today, still full of tranquility in spite of the intrusion of a twentieth century vehicle. The road in the foreground is an ancient one, known as The Normandy. History abounds here with ghosts of French monks, the old name of 'Hell Corner', and the deep well that once supplied the priest's house.

THEN – MILL BAY: This was the scene in about 1907, before the Garden of Remembrance had been laid out by local celebrity Nellie Laughton, in memory of her husband and others killed in the 1914-18 war. The date of the footbridge appears to be unknown, but it must have replaced earlier bridges, which probably took the place of a stone causeway across the river. Nearby were the Barrack Fields, which later became Horsham Cricket Ground (regiments were stationed here up to 1814).

NOW: The footbridge is still in use, but the view of the church has been covered by the trees. Mrs Laughton's garden is still giving delight, but is now maintained by Horsham District Council. Nellie Laughton is still remembered by older residents as the lady, usually dressed in black and white, who carried sugar laumps for the tradesmen's horses, and who gave the town its first ambulance.

THEN – SITE OF HORSHAM MARKET IN THE BISHOPRIC: The photograph dates from *c*1900. This was where the market flourished up to the 1920s, when it moved to the station yard. In 1910 the corn market was held every Wednesday, with poultry and cattle being sold on alternate Wednesdays. It was said that on market day almost every house in the Bishopric sold beer. The Green Dragon pub was originally an open frame house, with an internal well, discovered during modern alterations. This road was originally known as 'Archbishopric' from when the Archbishop of Canterbury owned lands here.

NOW: The Green Dragon is still there, having recently been renovated. The site of the old market has now become a beautiful water garden, and a favourite spot for open air dining.

THEN – THE BISHOPRIC AND HORSHAM'S FIRST CAR PARK: This was in the 1950s when the car park also boasted elegant public toilets and a waiting room for coach passengers. It was said that when the car park was first opened it was little used, as there was virtually no demand for car parking in the town.

NOW: The car park site is still used by cars, but now they are on the move in Albion Way at this busy junction. The only familiar landmark is the brewery chimney.

THEN – HOUSES IN THE BISHOPRIC: The picture is undated, but this was probably the late nineteenth century. Several local celebrities lived in the Bishopric, among them Mrs Smallwood the milk seller, who lived to be nearly 100, and up to her ninety-sixth year carried milk to her customers on a yoke suspended from her shoulders. There was also Henry Burstow who wrote his *Reminiscences of Horsham* in 1911, and who was famed as a folk singer and bell-ringer. The Bishopric was popularly known as The Rookery, although it was also sometimes called The Oxford Road, or Lower West Street. The earlier name was said to be either because of the many rooks in the Bishopric trees, or because residents behaved in a very noisy and 'rook-like' manner.

NOW: The old houses have completely disappeared, and new shops have taken their place. The annual Horsham in Bloom competition is the reason for the floral displays on the lamp posts. This is supported by traders and private residents, backed up by the district council.

THEN – HORSHAM GRAMMAR SCHOOL *c*1925: The school was founded by Richard Collyer in 1532. It moved from Denne Road to this site in 1893, and is now a sixth form college. For years the schoolboys in their distinctive uniforms, and the prefects with tassels on their caps, were a familiar sight in Hurst Road – obeying rules and staying on just one side of the road. The message on the back of this postcard reads: 'Dear Irene, I have gained the scholarship and this is the school I am going to. Give my love to your mother and father. Harold.' The date was June 22, l925. I hope Harold enjoyed his new school.

NOW: Not too many changes, at least from the outside, with just one oramental tower missing. The wooden gates have been replaced by metal ones, and there are additions to the building on the right hand side. However the pupils tend to look a little different.

COTTAGE HOSPITAL. HORSHAM.

THEN – HORSHAM COTTAGE HOSPITAL, HURST ROAD: This, Horsham's first hospital, opened in 1892, having cost less than £2,000 to erect. It is pictured in 1908. In 1923 it ceased to be a hospital when a much larger building was erected on the eastern side. This in turn has had major extensions since the 1980s. Some may remember the strict regime of the early days, when patients were said to have had to 'lay to attention' for the matron's inspection, although no doubt care and treatment were always the best available.

NOW: The building still remains, having changed little on the outside. Since it ceased to be a hospital, it has had many uses, mainly connected with medical care, although for a time it was in use as an addition to the Grammar School, opposite. Hurst Road was constructed in 1870, and named after a well known local family.

THEN – HORSHAM RAILWAY STATION: This is an undated picture, probably around 1900. The railway station was originally expected to be in Brighton Road; in fact a hotel was built there in expectation in 1834. Ultimately the first station was placed in the present goods yard area in 1848, when Horsham was still the 'end of the line'. In 1859 the line from Three Bridges was continued to Petworth, with a line to Guildford in 1865 and from Dorking in 1867. The second station (shown in this picture) was built in 1859 slightly south of the present station. In 1923 the London Brighton and South Coast Railway became part of Southern Railway, which was later absorbed into British Rail.

NOW: The present station, somewhat to the left of the earlier building. This was built in 1938 just missing the wartime period when building work was halted for the duration. The building carries its years well and is a pleasing example of 1930s railway architecture.

THEN – THE STATION HOTEL: The hotel is pictured in an advertisement of the 1930s. It was put up at about the same time as the first station, and served travellers and locals well, with a useful hall beside the main building.

NOW: The same building, but today a Beefeater Restaurant with adjoining travel lodges.

THEN – SHEP'S PAPER SHOP AT 60 NORTH STREET *c*1950s: This tiny shop, which was many times extended, was owned by Arthur Sheppard, and was very popular with commuters and others using the railway station. A regular visitor was a friendly horse owned by the urban district council, which insisted on entering the front section of the shop to obtain his daily sweet ration. The little shop was rather overwhelmed by the solid house on its right (number 58) lived in by Mrs Maud Mason in the 1950s.

NOW: A shiny modern shop building occupies the sight, but somehow it just doesn't have the character of Mr Sheppard's emporium.

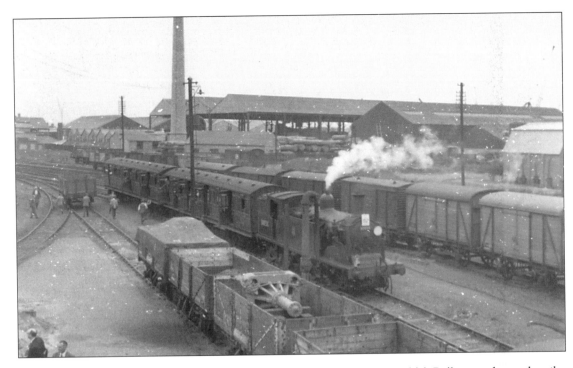

THEN – RAILWAY GOODS YARD: An undated picture but evidently in British Rail steam days, when the yard was a very busy place. There were three signal boxes at Horsham for several years, and the staff who worked in the yard were a very close-knit group. Those who lived near the yard may remember the detonators that were used on the line at midnight on New Years Eve. Some people complained, and apologies were always made, but somehow forgotten about by the following year.

NOW: The yard today, still recognisable but much less busy. Missing in this picture are the tall chimney and Agate's timber yard buildings. Also the locally famous crane, which was reputed to supply a weather forecast, if either upright or at rest.

THEN – CHART'S CORNER: Amos Chart's shop at the junction of Park Street and North Street *c*1910. He sold hay, straw, corn, coal, coke, lime, manure and gravel. When he took the children on an outing in one of his carts, they prayed for him in school the next day '*Our Father Chart in Heaven . . .*' Later the shop became Model Corner, but was finally demolished in 1988.

NOW: All that is left of Chart's Corner is the old house, although the walk-way which replaced the first section of North Street is now known as Chart Way. The buildings on either side belong to the Royal and Sun Alliance group of companies.

THEN – NORTH STREET: The view from Chart's Corner and the Hurst Arms *c*1910, leading down to the Carfax past St Mark's Church, which it was said had been built largely for the use of the servants whilst their lords and masters worshipped at the parish church of St Mary the Virgin. The Hurst Arms, on the right of the picture, appears to have attracted a large crowd, probably looking at the photographer.

NOW: The same view, now somewhat changed, with just the pub remaining on the right – today known as The Black Jug, which is an old name revived. The spire of St Marks may be seen on the left, but that is all, as the church itself has disappeared. At the north end of Chart Way there is now the Queen Victoria Jubilee Fountain, refurbished and with gas lighting, having been moved twice since it began life on the Carfax.

THEN – NORTH PARADE: The main road from the town to The Common area, and later becoming the Dorking-London route. This was in the early 1900s when the road was very rural, with parklands on either side. Even as late as the 1920s I can remember cattle and sheep being driven along this road, without anyone worrying about traffic. Walking down to church and the town from The Common, where I lived as a boy, this road seemed interminable, perhaps because there were no houses or other buildings.

NOW: The same view, still with many trees, but now adjuncts of modern living such as pedestrian lights and traffic bollards have been added. On the right is Horsham Park, and the grounds of the left have now become a splendid residential development.

THEN – ST LEONARD'S ROAD: The photograph dates from the early twentieth century. In spite of the houses this was almost the country, as far as Horsham was concerned. In fact surprise was expressed at houses being built so far from the centre of the town. There is a delightful group of children on the right of the picture, perhaps because there was a sweet shop close by.

NOW: The same view, still not too much changed, except for the road surface and the cars, and a lot more lamp standards.

THEN – TANBRIDGE HOUSE: This was after Tanbridge House had become the Horsham High School for Girls. In 1968 it was described as 'a fine example of the revived Wealden tradition'. The original Tanbridge House had been built in 1524, when it was known as Cadmans. It was bought by Thomas Oliver in 1860, but in 1887 the family moved to the present house, and the older one was demolished. The High School grounds have now become a well laid out development of houses and flats. Tan Bridge was one of Horsham's early bridges. Disputes over its upkeep erupted through the centuries, but in 1870 it became a county bridge and the payment of tolls came to an end.

NOW: Tanbridge House as it is today, converted to luxury apartments but with the exterior largely undisturbed.

THEN – THE DOG AND BACON PUB: The photograph dates from the early 1900s. The original hostelry had been in the cottage next to the pub. Here was the last bit of Horsham's common land before the enclosures. The name The Common still survives and refers to all the housing development around this part of the town. This was a popular stopping place for coaches in the revival of the 1900s, and also for charabancs in the 1930s. For a time there was a tea garden in front of the pub, with smartly dressed waitresses serving tea and cakes.

NOW: The Dog and Bacon is still popular today, although customers tend to arrive in cars rather than coaches or charabancs.

THEN – WARNHAM MILL *c*1900: This was once one of many mills in Horsham. My grandfather worked here in his younger days, and my father remembered playing beneath the bridge that carried the river under the road and into Warnham Pond. In the early years of this century winters appeared to be more severe. The pond (originally used by the iron makers) always seemed to be covered with ice and skaters appeared from all around the town. Floodgates were built in 1876, but were breached in 1906, causing a local sensation when the water level dropped in the pond and thousands of fish perished.

NOW: The mill, refurbished in the 1980s, and the mill wheel rebuilt and once again functioning.

ABOUT THE AUTHOR

Tony Wales was born in 1924 in Albion Terrace, Horsham – in a house and a street which no longer exist. He went to school in Horsham and Roffey, leaving at fourteen to work in an East Street ironmonger's shop.

Later, for nearly twenty years, he became press and publications officer of the English Folk Dance and Song Society at its London headquarters, Cecil Sharp House. Here he was responsible for scores of books on folk song and music, and collections of folk songs.

His interest in Sussex social history manifested itself in his first Sussex book, *We Wunt be Druv*, in 1976. This was followed over the years by around two dozen other Sussex titles, including *A Sussex Garland, The West Sussex Village Book, Sussex Ghosts and Legends, Landscapes of West Sussex* and several books of old Horsham pictures.

In 1999 he was presented with the Scan Tester Award for services to Sussex folk music. He has been chairman and president, and is now vice-president, of the Horsham Museum Society.

Bill Young is a former Lewes and Ringmer resident who now lives in Eastbourne. He is a retired local government officer who spent most of his career working for the emergency services – the Ambulance Services in Surrey and in Derbyshire and, latterly, the Fire Brigade in East Sussex where he ended his service as Assistant Chief Officer (Corporate Services). He was a founder member of the Ringmer History Group and, apart from local history, he counts fire brigade history, photography, classical and choral music among his interests.